modRNA 404

modRNA 404

Why It Matters & Other Essays

THOMAS RENZ

ATTRIBUTIONS
Interior Text Font: Minion Pro
Cover Design & Typesetting: Robbie W, Grayson III

BOOK PUBLISHER INFORMATION
RENZ MEDIA, LLC

TABLE OF CONTENTS

A Note
from the Publisher

The publisher is providing this book and its contents on an "as is" basis and makes no representations or warranties of any kind with respect to this book or its contents and disclaims all such representations and warranties, including but not limited to warranties of mental healthcare for a particular purpose.

The content of this book is for informational purposes only and is not intended to diagnose, treat, cure, or prevent any mental condition or disease. This book is not intended as a substitute for consultation with a licensed practitioner. Please consult with a physician or healthcare specialist regarding the suggestions and recommendations made in this book.

The Purpose
of This Book

This topic is pretty science heavy, so at this point I also want to acknowledge two additional points.

First, I am not a Peter McCullough—or a Harvey Risch-level scientist. I am a lawyer with some science background. That means that I am *not* the guy who will creates science. To do my job as an attorney by litigating in this area, however, I have to be able to read and understand the science. I do those two things quite well.

Second, the information I'm providing you in this little book is based simply on reading and understanding the science. I have not created anything here. I just know how to read, deduct, and explain.

Disclaimers aside, I want to open this topic with a confession. I originally titled this little book with the acronym *mRNA*, but that was intentionally misleading. For purposes of this book, *mRNA* actually stands for *modRNA* which is different from *mRNA* in two critical ways.

- mRNA is messenger RNA and found all over in every living organism.

- modRNA is laboratory-modified RNA that has been synthetically created for a purpose. It can be more durable and have substantially greater impact than a true mRNA as well as do many other things.

Why does this matter? Read on.

THOMAS RENZ
RENZ LAW

WHAT IS
modRNA
& WHY IT
MATTERS

Because mRNA is a weak particle and breaks down easily with a relatively lower risk of interfering with your genetics than other gene therapy products, (like modRNA) it is always *mRNA* that is being discussed in all conversations about the jabs. However, the problem is that it is a lie. Look at the FDA label for the Pfizer jab: you can find the entire label here.[1]

Note that different vials are denoted by their cap colors. But *also* notice that under number 3, one of the ingredients is *modRNA*. No one is talking about this, but it is crucial. Why?

The human body is built on instructions carried in our genes. What follows in is a great summary of this info from the NIH (National Institutes of Health).[2]

"

Life as we know it is specified by the genomes of the myriad organisms with which we share the planet. Every organism possesses a genome that contains the biological information needed to construct and maintain a living example of that organism.

Most genomes, including the human genome and those of all other cellular life forms, are made of DNA (deoxyribonucleic acid) but a few viruses have RNA (ribonucleic acid) genomes. DNA and RNA are polymeric molecules made up of chains of monomeric subunits called nucleotides.

To give you an idea of how compli-
cated the genes that make up our bodies
are, the following description from the
same webpage as previous follows.[3]

"

The human genome, which is typical of the genomes of all multicellular animals, consists of two distinct parts (Figure 1.1):

*The nuclear genome comprises approximately 3 200 000 000 nucleotides of DNA, divided into 24 linear molecules, the shortest 50 000 000 nucleotides in length and the longest 260 000 000 nucleotides, each contained in a different chromosome. These 24 chromosomes consist of 22 autosomes and the two sex chromosomes, X and Y.

*The mitochondrial genome is a circular DNA molecule of 16 569 nucleotides, multiple copies of which are located in the energy-generating organelles called mitochondria.

"

Each of the approximately 1013 cells in the adult human body has its own copy or copies of the genome, the only exceptions being those few cell types, such as red blood cells, that lack a nucleus in their fully differentiated state. The vast majority of cells are diploid and so have two copies of each autosome, plus two sex chromosomes, XX for females or XY for males - 46 chromosomes in all. These are called somatic cells, in contrast to sex cells or gametes, which are haploid and have just 23 chromosomes, comprising one of each autosome and one sex chromosome. Both types of cell have about 8000 copies of the mitochondrial genome, 10 or so in each mitochondrion.

So think about how complex that makes us: our bodies. The nuclear genome contains 3.2 billion nucleotides, and the mitochondrial genome contains 16.5 million. Each of these were designed by God and have evolved over millennia to work as a singular machine.

Now imagine an analog watch. The watch tells exact time because a complexity of tiny gears all work perfectly together to move each hand the appropriate amount to point to the proper hour, minute, and second. If one of these gears becomes damaged or the wrong gear is put in the wrong place, the watch would fail to achieve its function

While the most complex of watches might have hundreds of parts, our bodies have billions.

With that in mind let's talk about modRNA (or worse—*saRNA*). Rather than taking my word for what this is, let me share this explanation from Pfizer[3] until they change it (which will likely happen shortly after I publish this article).

So Pfizer's modRNA and saRNA vaccines modify the nucleosides that make up the genes that make up our bodies. Now consider this:

Windows 10 apparently has 50 million lines of code. Windows 11 has 60-100 million lines of code. Google has 2 billion lines of code.

Each operating system has more bugs in than any of us can fathom as demonstrated by the fact that everyone who uses a computer spends half of their time swearing at it. If we cannot make 50 million lines of code work right, why in the hell would we think we can insert random code into a product that is 3300 billion lines of code—many of which we do not fully understand—and not have problems?

Understand that at the core mRNA, modRNA, saRNA, etc. are *all* gene therapies and fundamentally designed for genetic manipulation. To suggest that this purpose is high risk is an understatement. We have no idea what we are doing, yet we continue forward trying to control these genes.

I want to apologize, but I do not want there to be any doubt that modRNA is all about gene editing. To make this point, I have to point to out some ugly "sciency" stuff.

Let me start with this abstract from an article titled "Genome Engineering for Stem Cell Transplantation."[4]

To avoid the ethical issues of embryonic stem cells, genome engineering has focused on inducible pluripotent stem cells, which can develop into all three germ layers. The ability to detect methylation patterns in these cells allows research into pluripotency markers.

The recently developed CRISPR system has allowed widespread application of genome engineering techniques. The CRISPR-Cas9 system, a potent system for genome editing, can be used for gene knockout or knock-in genome manipulations through substitution of a target genetic sequence with a desired donor sequence.

Two types of genome engineering can be initiated: homologous or nonhomologous DNA repair by the Cas9 nuclease. Delivery of the CRISPR-Cas9 and target donor vectors in human pluripotent stem cells can be accomplished via viral and nonviral delivery methods.

Nonviral delivery includes lipid-mediated transfection and electroporation. It has become the most common and efficient in vitro delivery method for human pluripotent stem cells.

The CRISPR-Cas9 system can be combined with inducible pluripotent stem cells to generate single or multiple gene knockouts, correct mutations, or insert reporter transgenes. Knockouts can also be utilized to investigate epigenetic roles and targets, such as investigation of DNA methylation. CRISPR could be combined with human pluripotent stem cells to explore genetic determinants of lineage choice, differentiation, and stem cell fate, allowing investigators to study how various genes or noncoding elements contribute to specific processes and pathways.

The CRISPR-Cas9 system can also be used to create null or nuclease dead Cas9, which has no enzymatic activity but has been utilized through fusion with other functional protein domains. In conclusion, RNA-guided genome targeting will have broad implications for synthetic biology, direct perturbation of gene networks, and targeted ex vivo and in vivo gene therapy.

For those of you who are human and think this reads like hieroglyphics, let me explain why it matters.

It is all about using the genetic modification of stem cells with various types of gene therapy.

The discussion about delivery methods, what they want to do with DNA, and the use of RNA are all related to modifying human genetics.

At some point this might become safe and effective, but at present *it is not even close.*

Further, note that the way this article talks about "RNA-guided genome targeting" and gene therapy means that there is acknowledgment that all we are seeing stems from the singular goal of controlling the human genome.

Since the time of that 2019 article, "science" has advanced. We now have several years of modRNA experimentation on billions of people around the world via the COVID vaccines, and the direction of this work has continued to evolve.

In 2022 an article was published titled "Robust genome editing via modRNA-based Cas9 or base editor in human pluripotent stem cells." It focused again on modifying human genetics by using modRNA.[5] That article has the following summary:

"

CRISPR systems have revolutionized biomedical research because they offer an unprecedented opportunity for genome editing.

However, a bottleneck of applying CRISPR systems in human pluripotent stem cells (hPSCs) is how to deliver CRISPR effectors easily and efficiently. Here, we developed modified mRNA (modRNA)-based CRISPR systems that utilized Cas9 and p53DD or a base editor (ABE8e) modRNA for the purposes of knocking out genes in hPSCs via simple lipid-based transfection.

ABE8e modRNA was employed to disrupt the splice donor site, resulting in defective splicing of the target transcript and ultimately leading to gene knockout. Using our modRNA CRISPR systems, we achieved 73.3% ± 11.2% and 69.6 ± 3.8% knockout efficiency with Cas9 plus p53DD modRNA and ABE8e modRNA, respectively, which was significantly higher than the plasmid-based systems. In summary, we demonstrate that our non-integrating modRNA-based CRISPR methods hold great promise as more efficient and accessible techniques for genome editing of hP-SCs.

In English this essentially describes how effective and efficient modRNA is at genome editing. Remember that all the COVID vaccines are gene therapy products, *and none are using natural mRNA.* Instead, each are toying with those 3300 billion lines of code that make humans work and hoping that there are no unintended consequences.

I know this is complex and that there is a lot to consider, but let me state that the biochemical modifications that have been done to RNA have altered it substantially. These alterations were done for the purpose of allowing the use of these various RNA technologies to modify the human genome. In light of the complexity of the human genome, not only do we have no idea of the consequences but I do not believe we can truly state which changes will ultimately be permanent and which will be temporary.

Further, the "progress" in RNA tech has not only gone toward creating more effective methods of altering the makeup of humanity, but it has also gone toward ensuring these gene therapies be more robust and last longer. While much of that discussion will be for another book, that is precisely the reason that they can now create foods that deliver gene therapy "vaccines" to people as well as other things (mosquitoes, aerosols, topicals, etc.).

These implications are quite clear. My research has been extensive though only a very small part of it is included here because most of the documents are so technical that they are nonsensical to people not used to reading them. That said, I challenge anyone to argue with what I have written.

Our genomes are ours. Those spearheading these efforts are dead set on remaking humanity in an image that is not God's and doing so without people even knowing that it's happening—let alone consenting.

I am not okay with this. While I understand that this may not make for a great talking point for our politicians on FOX, it is foundational to humanity.

The combination of the complexity of the topic and the bought-off politicians makes this topic something that many fear. But if we don't deal with it, we might end up being remade into something we do not recognize.

Is
mRNA
Evil?

Let me preface this article with the following:

- The COVID vaccines are neither safe nor effective. All should be removed from the market immediately;

- I am against any genetic treatments in human beings because we do not understand the entirety of the human genome. It seems imprudent to "reprogram" something we do not completely understand when we cannot write software from scratch without bugs;

- As a Christian, I believe we are created in the image of God. Intentionally modifying our own genetic makeup seems morally wrong to me.

While it is reasonable to say that mRNA could potentially be used for good without modifying human genes, the lies told throughout COVID have destroyed any faith I have in anyone within our federal regulatory system or within the pharmaceutical industry; and

Without entirely rebuilding the healthcare industry at this point (including the relevant regulatory bodies), there is zero chance of me accepting these potential poisons. That process will take many years before trust is restored.

Dr. Peter McCullough is a brilliant doctor and knows more about science than I could ever hope to learn in my lifetime. His work has encompassed decades. In my relatively frequent interactions with him, I have found him to be absurdly smart, very ethical, and one of the few doctors willing to stand for what is right rather than for what is easy.

He recently wrote an article on his Substack that I feel needs to be distinguished with some critical perspective.

McCullough's article, "The Novelty of mRNA Viral Vaccines and Potential Harms: A Scoping Review"[6-7] briefly discusses a journal article referencing mRNA vaccines, generally (as opposed to exclusively) focusing on the COVID rollout[8] Both McCullough and the article he discusses note that the COVID vaccines have essentially been a disaster. However, both also discuss the possibility that future vaccines based on mRNA tech have potential to be safe and effective.

While I am not qualified to argue with McCullough or the scientists involved in the journal article, I am more than qualified to pose some relevant questions that ought to be addressed.

Let me preface by presupposing that there are very few things in the world that are inherently good or evil. Based on my understanding of the science, the idea of inserting a messenger RNA particle into a human body to "train" the body to deal with a given disease is not inherently evil (I'm certain that statement might surprise some but let me explain).

Further, if created ethically, the messenger RNA concept actually makes sense as a viable solution for many health issues. This is where I think Peter's article (and the journal article) needs further consideration. The key issue stems from the universal truth that evil begets evil. Therefore, a product with the potential to cure simply becomes evil when created without an ethical foundation.

Created ethically and properly, mRNA would not alter human genetics but, rather, would simply show the human body how to produce a material that would mitigate a germ, virus, etc. When created improperly, it appears that this disastrous material might permanently alter human genetics, teaching the body to create dangerous pathogens and causing countless unintended consequences (or intended if you don't fully trust the Bill Gates, WEF, CCP crew). As is often the case, the things with the greatest potential for good also have the greatest potential for evil. Based on my research, the mRNA vaccines for COVID were not created ethically and are a disaster.

At this point we know a lot about what has happened in & around COVID and the mRNA vaccine rollout. The following are a few key points:

- The FDA lied when they said that the only side effects would be "redness & swelling at the injection site…" As of October 22, 2020 before the release of the vaccines, the FDA Advisory Committee was presented with a discussion of risks related to the vaccine. That presentation included THIS slide (include later):[9]

- Fauci, Birx, & literally everyone else that had access to approval data related to the COVID jabs lied nonstop for three years. Many are still lying. Birx admits that she is a liar—"Dr. Birx's Bombshell Vaccine Admission: "I Knew Vaccines Wouldn't Protect Against Infection."[10]

- On September 28, 2021 the ACIP crew were shown Project Salus, a Department of Defense summary of the chaos being caused by the poison OUR DOD was pushing on the American public. The following statements were made in that presentation (remember Sept 2021)[11]:

*"In this 80% vaccinated >=65 population, an estimated 71% of COVID-19 cases occurred in fully vaccinated individuals"

*"In this 80% vaccinated 65+ population, an estimated 60% of COVID-19 hospitalizations occurred in fully vaccinated individuals in the week ending August 7th"

*"Risk of breakthrough hospitalization increases with time elapsed since mRNA vaccination with odds ratio increasing to 2.5 at 6 months post vaccination"

The possibility of these mRNA jabs "shedding" or transmitting to others without any notice or consent was real. Along with the fact that contact between a vaccinated person and a pregnant person was a reportable safety event in an early Pfizer study, the FDA requested and Pfizer agreed to perform a study on shedding as part of the approval process for Cominarty (which was never manufactured). Pfizer never even tested to determine if the vaccines would prevent infection. [12]

The Pfizer vaccines appear to destroy your immune system: The BNT162b2 mRNA vaccine against SARS-CoV-2 reprograms both adaptive and innate immune responses.

It goes on and on. While it would take four books worth of Substack space to list all the lies told about the COVID jabs, the point is that there is simply no longer any trust. The trust issue is compounded by the fact that it appears more realistic every day that these jabs might be altering human DNA through a process known as reverse transcriptase.

This study shows that mRNA can alter human DNA, and this information was also part of at least one ACIP briefing.[13]

In light of the fact that everything about the COVID vaccines has been a lie and in light of the fact that these mRNA products do appear to be able to permanently alter human genetics, I think it is crucial that we recognize that any drug that could possibly impact our genetics (mRNA or otherwise) is something that many will not take. Further, I think that in light of the bad faith demonstrated throughout the pandemic, many will lose faith or at least become more reticent to continue with known vaccines. After all, why trust that the pharmaceutical companies that have lied every step of the way would not alter existing vaccines, especially as it is common knowledge that there are plans in the works to replace all vaccines with mRNA as well as to create hundreds more?

Peter was right as he has always been on the science here, but I'd love his take on the ethics and impact. At the end of the day, when do you trust a liar? For me the answer is never. The vaccine pushers have continued to lie and are now even pushing vaccines into food.[14]

If we start getting actual truth and facts, we can begin rebuilding trust. At this point, however I do not see that happening without substantial legislation being passed and people being held accountable for the deaths these lies have caused. Until then, while mRNA might have promise, there's simply no way that thinking people will trust it.

mRNA
Is in
Food

Bad news: the Big Pharma complex wants to hide vaccines in your food including these mRNA poisons. Good news: *Missouri HB1169 could stop this.* Best news: other states are considering similar bills to protect the food supply

I want to begin this article with some background. First of all, yes, vaccines can be made transmissible through food. Second, mRNA IS in the food supply already. Third, it appears the vaccines may, in fact, actually alter your DNA permanently. And Fourth, regardless of whether the mRNA in the food supply or that which is about to be authorized for the food supply is transmissible, we have no way of know it is safe unless you want to trust the same people that told you the COVID jabs were safe and effective (despite the fact that they did not test to determine if the jabs prevented transmission and have admitted they do not understand the immune response mechanism).

Here are the categories for the citations to this article in the *Citations* page at the end of this book:

- Vaccines can be Transmissible[15]
- Controlling Epidemics with Transmissible Vaccines[16-18]
- Transmitting to Livestock Through[19-20]
- mRNA Vaccine Transmissible through Cow Milk[21-22]
- mRNA IS in the Food Supply Already[23]
- Merck-Animal-Health-Statement-on-SEQUIVITY-Technology[24-]

- Merck mRNA Vaccines - Sequivity[25]
- Bayer and BioNTech Partner to create mRNA jabs[26]
- mRNA being used in Australian Cattle (no country of origin labeling in America means it is here as well)[27]
- Vaccines May Permanently Alter DNA (This Study Shows That mRNA CAN Alter Human DNA)[28]

Given the massive holes in our knowledge gaps and the number of lies regarding the safety and efficacy of mRNA vaccines it is difficult to know or trust that meat treated with these vaccines is safe. Remember Fauci and crew telling us this was a "crisis of the unvaxxed" and that the hospitals were filled to capacity with 90%+ of the patients being unvaxxed? That while he had the DoD data from Project Salus showing the exact opposite.

While I will not suggest anyone should simply "trust what I'm saying" I will tell you that in numerous conversations with scientists investigating the issue, I am consistently hearing that when they test, they are finding mRNA in the food supply already. In fact, within the last week I was shown data and microscopy demonstrating this to be true (I saw the images of the microscopy myself). These are not public (to my knowledge) but I hope to share the information as it becomes available to publicly disseminate.

Despite the immense evidence of mRNA already being in the food supply, I'm certain the pro-vax crew will try. That said, it simply cannot be denied that there are an immense number of gene therapy vaccines under development for use in food in the immediate future. Further, as shown above, the manufacturers of these gene altering poisons are also creating plants with transmissible vaccines. A fundamental issue facing the public in this is that this new capacity to create ingestible vaccines that potentially alter our genetics is that the law is woefully inadequate to deal with this technology.

The law governing gene altering food was written before the capacity to reprogram peoples' genome with food was possible, so it simply did not address it. There are considerable loopholes and legitimate questions about disclosure. Further, given the corruption we are seeing in the federal government (especially related to the world of Big Pharma), it would seem to be unwise to trust them for enforcement.

All this leads to Missouri HB1169: the only solution to the issue we have at the moment.[29] State Representative Holly Jones has sponsored HB1169 and I think the response really tells us how important it is to pass. The bill, as introduced, did three things:

- It required disclosure if any product was going to modify your genetics or act as a gene therapy product (this included food);

- It allowed people request information about how any gene therapy products could be spread or transmitted to others that had not consented to taking it; and

- It required fully informed consent (all risks and benefits including adverse events of special interest) prior to someone being given any medical intervention or gene therapy product.

This simple bill was about two pages long and easy enough to read that anyone could understand it. Despite these very simple goals, the elected officials of Missouri were quite split on the bill. The most surprising objections came from Republicans that claimed (incorrectly) that it would cause problems for farmers and ranchers.

You are welcome to read through my Twitter profile if you'd like to further rehash the nonsense related to this bill and my response but ultimately Rep Jones and the other officials working with her to promote this bill decided to restructure a bit to address the complaints (which were simply regurgitations of the talking points given by the lobbyists—most of whom have direct ties to Big Pharma and Bill Gates/CCP factory farms).[30]

The text of the updated bill is here.[31] The updated language specifically excludes farmers and ranchers from the disclosure requirements while ensuring that food buyers are going to be informed if the food is a gene therapy or medical intervention. Specifically, you will see the following clause on the second page of this one-and-a-half page bill.[32]

Farmers and ranchers not in the business of creating or engineering gene therapy products or products intended to or known to alter a person's genome more substantially than natural food are exempt from the provisions of this section.

I received a number of questions about this and thought we should explain it. This section allows small farmers and ranchers that are given GMO products to know that they must be informed if the product they are using is going to turn their plants/animals into a drug or intervention. They can still choose to purchase or use the product and resellers would be responsible for informing consumers in that scenario.

This is very important for small farmers and ranchers. As it stands, the small farmers and ranchers may be buying the "best seed" or "best livestock" but that product could potentially act as a gene therapy and the farmer/rancher may never know. This would mean that if these new gene therapy products end up causing cancer ten years from now the small farmers could be liable for putting this out without even realizing they are doing it. Passage of this law would allow the farmers/ranchers to decide whether they want to use such products and would ensure the consumer knew what they were buying which would help protect the farmers/ranchers from lawsuits.

A number of trade associations claiming to care about farmers and ranchers are telling people that this is somehow a bad thing. The new language in the bill specifically creates exemptions for the farmers and ranchers so there should no longer be any objection to the law unless these guys are actually not truly representing the farmers/ranchers and rather, are simply looking out for their funders (Bayer, Merck, etc.). You see the huge factory farms are all owned by Bill Gates, CCP-controlled companies, or massive corporations controlled by BlackRock, Vanguard, etc. All these groups also have interests in Big Pharma, and this is a way to pad their pockets on multiple investments with a single move (gene therapies in food).

The bill still requires disclosure (with the farmer/rancher exemption) and still requires fully informed consent. It also, per the request of some GOP holdouts, includes a criminal charge for failing to provide informed consent. To move this bill forward the Representatives pushing this had no choice but to drop the transmissibility disclosure but the bill is still a major step in the right direction.

Ultimately this bill is now one-and-a-half pages long and literally has nothing to object to unless you oppose informed consent. This bill is incredibly easy to read, reduces the risk of lawsuits against farmers and ranchers, and ensures people will know if what they are going to eat will alter their genetic makeup. What is there to oppose? More importantly, if no one is putting gene therapies or other medical interventions in food why would *anyone* oppose this?

ADDENDUM
7 CFR § 205-603[33]

"SYNTHETIC SUBSTANCES ALLOWED FOR USE IN ORGANIC LIVESTOCK PRODUCTION ADDENDUM"

Even before this little book reached the printer, the powers have exploited a loophole in the law that affects the food supply. It allows that if a cow or pig (livestock) gets an mRNA vaccine (read, modRNA), a gene therapy, they can still be called organic. Your organic food can still be subject to gene therapies that are transmissable to humans because there is a loophole for vaccines. if it changes their DNA or is transmissible to humans, or is still in their system, you can be getting that in and through your organic food.

CITATIONS

1. https://labeling.pfizer.com/ShowLabeling.aspx?id=14471.

2. https://www.ncbi.nlm.nih.gov/books/NBK21134/:

3. https://www.pfizer.com/science/innovation/mrna-technology

4. https://doi.org/10.6002/ect.mesot2018.l34 (link to the full article is there as well).

5. https://www.ncbi.nlm.nih.gov/pmc/articles/PMC9499999/

6-7. "The Novelty of mRNA Viral Vaccines and Potential Harms: A Scoping Review" https://petermcculloughmd.substack.com/p/the-novelty-of-mrna-viral-vaccines?utm_source=post-email-title&publication_id=1119676&post_id=115415754&isFreemail=true&utm_medium=email
8. Halma, M.T.J.; Rose, J.; Lawrie, T. "The Novelty of mRNA Viral Vaccines and

Potential Harms: A Scoping Review." J 2023, 6, 220-235. https://doi.org/10.3390/j6020017.

9. FDA Advisory Committee (TBI)

10. "Dr. Birx's Bombshell Vaccine Admission: "I Knew Vaccines Wouldn't Protect Against Infection" (westernjournal.com) [9]

11. Salus Humetrix Ve Study Pdf

12. The slides here are from my own presentation at the ReAwakening Tour from September of 2021. All original documents are saved offline in the event the cites no longer work. For the Fact Checkers—I recommend you request the release of these study results before deciding the validity of the claim.

13. Aldén M, Olofsson Falla F, Yang D, Barghouth M, Luan C, Rasmussen M, De Marinis Y. Intracellular Reverse Transcription of Pfizer BioNTech COVID-19 mRNA Vaccine BNT162b2 In Vitro in Human Liver Cell Line. Curr Issues Mol Biol. 2022 Feb 25;44(3):1115-1126. doi: 10.3390/cimb44030073. PMID:

35723296; PMCID: PMC8946961.

14. https://fox5sandiego.com/news/coronavirus/volunteers-sought-for-trial-of-new-plant-based-covid-19-vaccine/

15. Bull JJ, Smithson MW, Nuismer SL. Transmissible Viral Vaccines. Trends Microbiol. 2018 Jan;26(1):6-15. doi: 10.1016/j.tim.2017.09.007. Epub 2017 Oct 13. PMID: 29033339; PMCID: PMC5777272.

16. Nuismer SL, May R, Basinski A, Remien CH (2018) Controlling epidemics with transmissible vaccines. PLOS ONE 13(5): e0196978. https://doi.org/10.1371/journal.pone.0196978

17. Bull JJ, Smithson MW, Nuismer SL. Transmissible Viral Vaccines. Trends Microbiol. 2018 Jan;26(1):6-15. doi: 10.1016/j.tim.2017.09.007. Epub 2017 Oct 13. PMID: 29033339; PMCID: PMC5777272.

18. Article from Grain.org: https://grain.org/e/245

19. FeedTitle: Vaccines in your salad? Scientists growing medicine-filled plants

to replace injections (https://communit-
yhubb.org/vaccines-in-your-salad-scien-
tists-growing-medicine-filled-plants-to-re-
place-injections/)

20. Rybicki EP. Plant-made vaccines for
humans and animals. Plant Biotechnol J.
2010 Jun;8(5):620-37. doi: 10.1111/j.1467-
7652.2010.00507.x. Epub 2010 Mar 11.
PMID: 20233333; PMCID: PMC7167690.

21. mRNA IS Transmissible Through
Breastmilk: Hanna N, Heffes-Doon A,
Lin X, et al. Detection of Messenger RNA
COVID-19 Vaccines in Human Breast
Milk. JAMA Pediatr. 2022;176(12):1268–
1270. doi:10.1001/jamapediat-
rics.2022.3581

22. Title: Grow and Eat Your Own Vaccines? Using Plants As mRNA Factories

23. mRNA IS in the Food Supply Already
24. Merck-Animal-Health-Statement-on-SEQUIVITY-Technology

25. Merck mRNA Vaccines - Sequivity

26. Bayer and BioNTech Partner to create mRNA jabs[26]

27. mRNA being used in Australian Cattle (no country of origin labeling in America means it is here as well)[27]

28. Aldén M, Olofsson Falla F, Yang D, Barghouth M, Luan C, Rasmussen M, De Marinis Y. Intracellular Reverse Transcription of Pfizer BioNTech COVID-19 mRNA Vaccine BNT162b2 In Vitro in Human Liver Cell Line. Curr Issues Mol Biol. 2022 Feb 25;44(3):1115-1126. doi: 10.3390/cimb44030073. PMID: 35723296; PMCID: PMC8946961.

29. Missouri HB1169

30. Thomas Renz Twitter

31. The updated language of Missouri HB1169

32. The second page of Missouri HB1169

33. 7 CFR § 205-603 https://twitter.com/Renz-Tom/status/1694320951444337038/photo/1

Thomas Renz is a prominent American Attorney, Political Commentator, Educator, Advocate, Businessman & Patriot. Tom has gained international attention for his work challenging pandemic-related policies and vaccine mandates, and advocating for individual liberties, medical freedom, and informed choice. Renz's legal expertise and relentless advocacy have established him as a leading voice in the fight for our Freedoms.

Printed in the USA
CPSIA information can be obtained
at www.ICGtesting.com
LVHW031527031123
762986LV00053B/1204